The Coati Kid: Surf Tales from Matapalo

Rick Hardy

Thanks to my own three amigos,
Clay, Dave, and Jacob,
for the inspiration to write
The Coati Kid,
and to all the others who helped along the way, especially
my wife, Darcy, for her editing and moral support.

January 2024

Chapter One

As Pollo reluctantly stepped upon the sands of Playa Pan Dulce in Cabo Matapalo, Costa Rica, he looked across the water toward his beloved Pavones, and sighed. Everything he understood about surfing was about to change. He was now on the Peninsula de Osa and everything was different on this side of the Golfo Dulce.

Pollo looking across Golfo Dulce toward his beloved Pavones

Pollo felt lost in this new community of right-handers, where the waves were all rights.

Pavones, and the beautiful left-handers, seemed a million miles away, even though it was just across the gulf. All the surfers on the Pavones' side respected Pollo, and most of them surfed like he did, with their right foot forward, which surfers call "goofy foot." The goofy footers never did quite understand what was so goofy about the way they stood on their surfboards, but such is life.

Pollo, going frontside, surfing goofy foot at Pavones

The majority of the surfers on the Matapalo side, at least those who rode traditional surfboards, were "regular foot" and surfed the rights with their left foot forward. While this seemed strange to Pollo, he was still eager to join his new

4

community of surfers and he dreamed of the first time he would ride regular foot on a right-hander.

Pollo dreaming of his first right-hander as a regular foot.

Since his arrival in Matapalo, Pollo had noticed three surfers in particular (who would become known as the Three Amigos) as they shredded Matachanchos. He was very excited about finding out who they were, as he dreamed of surfing as a regular foot.

The Three Amigos longboarding

While Matapalo's traditional surfers (those who rode surfboards) were totally awesome, some of the other types of surfers were equally amazing, including the "surfers of the air." Surfers of the air were neither goofy foot nor regular foot because they surfed a multidimensional medium—the air. These air surfers were capable of participating in the ultimate dance, utilizing the currents and wind patterns above Matapalo to create beautiful lines and extravagant patterns.

Darren was one of the most spectacular of the air surfers. With his large colorful beak, Darren surfed through the canopy of the bosque, always looking for a great ride while searching for a little snack.

Darren

Julian and Stu, two of the smoothest air surfers, were always up for a good morning session. Their skillful maneuvering, mere inches above the surface of the wave, was truly awe-inspiring.

Julian

Stu

While out surfing, Stu and Julian were always looking for a bait ball, and this is why they were so highly revered in the area. When Julian and Stu were flying around, dive bombing the rippled surface, everyone came running to the water's edge to enjoy the feeding frenzy. Where there's bait, there's often game fish, which was good for Stu, good for Julian, good for everyone!

Julian and Stu divebombing a bait ball

Another smooth air surfer, Texas Charlie, was a great friend of Stu's, and was also a great fisherbird. He was long and lean and was often seen soaring high above the beaches of Matapalo while looking for schools of fish. This cool bird was especially known for his uncanny way of fishing. Yes, Texas Charlie was certainly capable of divebombing a school of unsuspecting fish from his towering perspective, high above the water's surface, but he had also taught himself how to fish with a conventional rod and reel. This was quite a sight, and many could not believe their eyes when Texas Charlie was finessing the elusive Snook out of the mouth of the Tamales River.

Texas Charlie had lost the use of one of his legs, but he didn't let that interfere with his fishing. He fabricated a telescopic, prosthetic leg and this allowed multi-depth fishing whether the tide was high or low.

Texas Charlie landing a big Snook at the Tamales River mouth

Other surfers, like Mr. Bagley, Hippie Jim, and Phil, usually surfed beneath the surface of the water. Their powerful flippers propelled them smoothly and silently through the underwater currents, where they carved the cleanest of lines, with no wasted speed or energy.

Mr. Bagley, a very wise and talented turtle, was considered the master of technique and follow-through. When he wanted to learn a new skill, he stuck with it until he achieved mastery. Recently, he has taken up foiling, a water artform not practiced by many. He rode a special surfboard with a hydrofoil that lifted him above the surface of the water as the airplane-like wing caught the circular underwater motion of the incoming wave.

Mr. Bagley

He was often seen slicing through the early morning glass along the shores of Playa Pan Dulce. Mr. Bagley was highly revered within the Matapalo Beach community and drew respect and esteem from all.

Mr. Bagley foiling the early morning glass at Pan Dulce

Hippie Jim was a younger turtle but was still highly revered as a smooth underwater surfer, and he, like Mr. Bagley, yearned for new opportunities to ride the waves. Jim was perfecting a radical surfing stunt, "the stash and slash," which utilized a traditional surfboard in a way never seen before.

Hippie Jim

Phil, one of the most laidback of the underwater surfers, has been carving clean lines for decades in the waters of Matapalo, and is considered one of the pillars of the community after having the vision and drive to create Bosque del Cabo. His entrepreneurial spirit brought him to the Osa, and his drive and follow-through allowed him to stay.

Phil

Leo was a classic underwater surfer who knew how to catch the wave's energy without the use of a surfboard. He wasn't often seen, but when he was spotted, tips up, gliding through the water, everyone enjoyed his presence. Leo was one of the older surfers in Matapalo and was well liked by everyone.

Leo

There were several other traditional surfers besides the Three Amigos who Pollo had spotted shredding Matachanchos when he first arrived in Matapalo. These other amazing individuals came in all shapes and sizes and were from all kinds of diversified cultures and backgrounds, and they all loved Matapalo.

Yoga Charlie was one of the most unpretentious of the traditional board surfers around Matapalo. While technically being a bird, Yoga Charlie was not an "air surfer" mainly because he couldn't fly very well.

Yoga Charlie

He was so laidback that he perfected the "no-paddle" takeoff. This was truly something to see to believe.

Yoga Charlie's "no-paddle" takeoff

Hippie Jim, the cap wearing turtle, who was always up for a ceremony, was learning to ride a traditional surfboard, and had combined his underwater skills with some exciting surface shenanigans to perform his infamous "stash and slash."

Jim had mastered this crazy stunt by positioning his surfboard, floating perfectly in the line-up, awaiting his explosive antics. He would stash his board in the trough of an incoming wave and time it perfectly while waiting for his board to be sucked up the face. Jim would swim furiously beneath the water's surface and explode out of the water, landing perfectly on his board, propelling it down the rapidly cresting face. It wasn't the laidback "no-paddle" takeoff developed by Yoga Charlie, but it still demanded great respect!

Hippie Jim performing the incredible "Stash and Slash"

Felipe, Colorado Chris, and Koji were three cool cats who had perfected the art of surfing in the waters of Matapalo and while well respected in the bosque, these rain forest dwellers were also considered three of the best of the board surfers and all three had forged some great friendships out in the line-up.

Colorado Chris

Chris smiled as he thought of one such friendship and chuckled to himself when he recalled the secret arrangement he had with his little buddy Longboard Rick, one of his main snacks while hunting in the forest. In the water, Chris and Rick were the best of friends, but when not surfing,

Rick could be seen hopping through the bosque looking much like a bouncing football, keeping a keen eye out for predators, especially black panthers.

Longboard Rick

In the water, Chris allowed Rick to paddle into waves with him, understanding it would look like Rick was "dropping in" on him. The other surfers in the lineup were shocked at Rick's bold moves and always reacted in surprise as the two appeared to surf in complete synchronicity with one another and with the waves as well.

Chris felt this arrangement was actually making him a better surfer. While Rick was strictly "A to B," Chris was back in the hook, utilizing everything in his bag of tricks to remain stable, negotiating the most critical part of the wave. This secret arrangement worked wonderfully for Chris and Rick as they surfed twice as many waves in complete harmony. The other surfers were completely baffled.

Longboard Rick surfing with Colorado Chris

Koji was a smaller cat who was well known for surfing larger waves at Hog Hole. When Koji wasn't surfing, he attended to the needs of his local Matapalo surf crew and tourists at Blue Osa. Koji had perfected the artform of accuCLAWture and was highly revered on the Osa for his healing touch.

Koji

Pollo watched as his mother flew overhead and circled silently, carving beautiful lines in the baby blue sky above Matapalo. Her husband's capture by poachers during the last breeding season still hung heavy in her heart. Yet, even in her sadness, she had dreams of a new life for herself, as well as for her son Pollo and Gretchen (Pollo's wife), in the land of the right-handers.

Pollo's MOM

Pollo's wife, Gretchen

At that very moment, Gretchen fluttered by with the hypnotic stutter-flap of her delicate blue wings and landed on Pollo's nose. All three were happy to be together on the Peninsula de Osa.

Pollo's MOM watching as Gretchen lands on Pollo's nose

Chapter Two

Mr. Bagley was one of the oldest and wisest surfers on this side of Golfo Dulce. Similar to the surfers of the air, Mr. Bagley, when he wasn't foiling, carved clean lines beneath the water's surface without a surfboard. With his great understanding of tidal movement, swell size and direction, as well as proper "line-up" location, Mr. Bagley majestically measured his own surfing through continuity of energy, grace, skill, and most importantly, style. He glided through the beautiful blue waters of the right-handers as effortlessly as Pollo's mother flew overhead, enveloped in the majestic skies above Backwash Bay.

Pollo's mom and Mr. Bagley were of one spirit, simply expressing their love for life through different mediums—Pollo's mother surfed the skies, while Mr. Bagley carved graceful lines in the waters of Matapalo.

Darren flew by with a small iguana in his mouth, signaling breakfast time. Darren was the epitome of a surfer, tall and lean with chiseled features. His magnificently foiled beak enabled him to slice through the thick jungle air while making radical cutbacks and explosive aerials. Although getting on in years, Darren was still capable of catching his fair share of great rides and never seemed to miss the opportunity to grab a little snack. It wasn't widely known, but Darren was an omnivore, which was partly responsible for his great physique and his beautiful outlook on life.

Darren enjoying breakfast

B.D. was another spectacular air surfer who had been surfing for decades in the Matapalo area. He was one of the first to establish an eco-lodge in Matapalo that became known as Encanta la Vida and has been a favorite gathering place for decades. B.D. was known for some hilarious shenanigans and was once seen dressed up in a military uniform flying around the bosque. When improper surfer etiquette ensued, he would drop the proverbial "bomb" right on the subjects at large.

B.D. dropping a bomb

B.D., in a light-hearted way, was able to command dignity and respect while keeping the lineup a peaceful and orderly place. The way B.D. surfed the air, he looked like he was going to lose it at any moment and come crashing to earth, yet somehow, he always pulled it off. He was always in the most critical part of the maneuver, even while surfing somewhat erratically.

Pollo was forming friendships with many of the positive surfers on the Matapalo side, both surfers of the water (traditional and nontraditional) and surfers of the air. Pollo was also fashioning a friendship with the three spectacular surfers he had first spotted surfing Matachanchos upon his arrival.

The Three Amigos, Kaliman, Aaron, and Simón, surfed together when the waves were big and clean, and always enjoyed surfing together when Matachanchos was going off. They often enjoyed a good session at Backwash when the surf at Matachanchos wasn't working.

Kaliman was the smallest of the trio, but he surfed the largest of waves. Kaliman was known for his fearlessness while often surfing Matachanchos by himself. Kaliman has lived and worked in the Matapalo area for decades, dating back to the days of Tri-Pod... but that's a whole other story.

Kaliman

Kaliman surfing solo at Matachanchos

Aaron surfed for Carton Surfboards, and he was well known for his aggressive surf style, good looks and fabulous head fur. With his ability to attack the lip while looking for clean aerials, Aaron was a real crowd pleaser. He was also known for his fancy footwork on the dance floor at Martina's on Friday nights.

Aaron

Speaking of Martina...what can we say about this amazing female. Well, to start with, she is a pillar of the community, owning and operating Martina's Bar and Restaurant for over two decades, offering a fun and comfortable place to eat, drink and possibly dance the night away. Friday nights are magical! Just ask Aaron.

Martina, owner and operator of Martina's Bar and Restaurant

Simón, who was born and raised in Matapalo, had
moved on, but often came back for a clean south
swell. Simón was best known for his clean lines
and connectivity of turns. With Simón, there was
no wasted energy—everything flowed, and every
turn was seamlessly connected.

Simón

The Three Amigos not only enjoyed each other's company, they also fed off each other's egos, egging on larger wave selection and more radical maneuvers, from deeper tube riding to more explosive aerials.

The Three Amigos shredding Matachanchos

Mako, however, was one surfer who was not a favorite of Pollo's. Yes, his name was that of a shark, and this was very appropriate. Mako, you see, had a reputation as someone who was not to be trusted. He was known to play tricks on tourists, which often resulted in the loss of funds—and sometimes worse. His reputation on the beach often followed him into the lineup, where he regularly paddled to the peek and oftentimes paddled behind the deepest surfer, only to snake him or her. (No offense, Andy.)

Mako

Mako had his share of followers, and this helped create total havoc for Pollo. Mako's groms thought Mako was simply the bomb and they followed him blindly, willing to disrupt the lineup by snaking people or dropping in on deeper surfers.

Matapalo was slowly becoming the pinnacle of Pollo's existence. However, there were problems on the beach, as well as in the water, and most often this occurred when Mako and his groms would crowd the peak and cause undue stress. Pollo witnessed all of this from the beach and frowned in disgust. He couldn't wait to be out in the water, but for now he was still unsure of his abilities on the new right-handers.

Although Pollo had never surfed a right-hander, he knew that one day, he would carve graceful lines in the majestic blue waters of Matapalo, just like his new friends, the Three Amigos.

Mr. Bagley sensed that something was troubling Pollo, and one starry night, the wise sea turtle approached a small group of surfers on the beach. He beckoned the young coatimundi for a private conversation. Mr. Bagley, getting straight to the point, questioned Pollo about his despondent, faraway gaze.

"*Polloson*, (little Pollo), what is the matter?" the old turtle asked.

Mr. Bagley questioning Pollo

Pollo wiped away a few tears and mumbled, "I long to carve graceful lines, but I have never surfed a right-hander."

Mr. Bagley, along with Aaron and Kaliman, showed their support for Pollo, and reassured him that they would soon be carving smooth and connected turns together.

Most of the surfers ignored Mako and his

groms, and mainly just wanted everyone in the lineup to follow proper surfer etiquette—taking turns and always "hooting" for friends as well as for strangers.

Pollo, with his eyes glazed over, remembered the beautiful left-handers that he and his mother had left behind, where he used to surf such breaks as Sawmills, Pilon, Wheelchairs, and the legendary Pavones point break at the Rio Claro River mouth, which were *all* left-handers.

Now, he was on the "other side," and was expected to surf in the waters of the right-handers, but Pollo had never surfed a right-hander.

All the surfers from Mako's gang mocked Pollo's goofy foot style, and this made him even more reluctant to paddle out into the lineup. When Mako's groms hurled insults at Pollo, B.D. would often fly by and drop a little bomb, if you know what I mean.

Overall, Pollo was well liked in Matapalo, but he still lacked the knowledge and confidence to paddle into a right-hander.

Chapter Three

It was Mr. Bagley who knew exactly what Pollo needed to do, and he was simply waiting for the young Coati Kid to come to him again.

Mr. Bagley had created a personalized training program for Pollo and was just waiting for him to reach out. He would train the Coati Kid in the basics of surfing the right-handers, emphasizing style and grace while continuously focusing on tidal movement, wind conditions, triangulation, as well as swell size and direction.

The Coati Kid

In Mr. Bagley's mind, the main emphasis for surfing should be beauty and style, with the surfer focusing on clean lines and smooth transitions. Mr. Bagley would instruct Pollo to gracefully approach the new directional energy of the right-handers, but first the Coati Kid had to learn and master the fundamentals.

Meanwhile, even though Pollo had yet to paddle out, Mako continued to make an issue of Pollo's goofy foot style at every opportunity. Pollo's reluctance to enter the lineup provided great fodder for Mako and his disciples, as they laughed at Pollo and made sport of him. Mako always did his best to belittle Pollo in front of the other surfers, but this was beginning to backfire.

Pollo had committed to a peaceful existence and never fell prey to Mako's callous remarks. He simply shined it on and continued with his daily activities, all the while yearning to surf circles around Mako in the challenging waters of Backwash Bay. Sometimes, the Coati Kid even dreamed that he and Mako would one day compete together in a surf contest.

Best of all, Pollo was continuing to make more friends, and this would prove to be beneficial in the lineup. Among them, Pollo had befriended the most lethal surfer in Matapalo. His name was Andy.

Andy

Andy was one of the deadliest creatures of the wooded bosque but was well known as a playful little guy who was often accused of "snaking" Mako in the lineup. With a few powerful shakes of his tail, Andy could jettison himself deeper in the pocket and basically rob Mako of any wave he chose to ride. Just the sound of Andy's tail shake was enough to totally rattle Mako. Pollo received great joy from Andy's antics.

Andy "snaking" Mako

Andy and Pollo had become friends on the beach, and the Coati Kid quickly realized that a friend like

Andy was always good to have on his side. Even though he was fun-loving and enjoyed slithering in and out of a healthy bush from time to time, Andy could take anyone down with just one hissing strike.

Two of the older surfers had been friends for a long time. Stu and Leo first met back in the 1950s, off the coast of California. They now took great pleasure in enjoying the fruits of their labor earned during what is considered the golden age of surfing. Back then, Stu had been surfing along, inches *above* the surface of a breaking wave, when he peered through the face of the wave and saw Leo gliding along, inches *below* the surface. Both were *using* the power of the wave, without actually surfing *on* the wave.

Leo was majestic in his approach to surfing, and his extremely large surface area allowed him to channel the energy of the wave while surfing the rolling energy with little to no effort. Stu had mastered the art of surfing the "air-wave" that was created on top of the surface by the cresting energy of an incoming swell.

Leo and Stu meeting for the first time in California in the 1950's

Mr. Bagley swam onto the beach after enjoying a delicious breakfast of sardines, crabs, and a small snapper, when he noticed a few of the surfers on the beach. He approached the group and took Pollo aside. He asked, "*Polloson*, do you wish to surf these new right-handers with style and grace?"

Mr. Bagley questioning Pollo

Pollo nodded with uncontrolled excitement, smiling and dreaming of carving clean, graceful lines like the other great surfers of Matapalo.

Everyone on the beach had overheard Mr. Bagley's question, and the Three Amigos, along with Chris and Darren, nodded in agreement. Pollo could certainly master the right-handers. Chris smiled as he thought about Pollo plugging into the new directional energy, and chuckled softly to himself, knowing how much Mako would fume and fuss.

Just then, Derek swam by, making a few fantastic jumps and several loud tail slaps to demonstrate his approval. When the surf was up, Derek would swim through the lineup, catching the set wave of the day. His jumps were spectacular, and the surfers of Matapalo enjoyed his show. When he finished a great ride, he would often blow a little tune through his blowhole.

Derek

Best of all, he would often discipline surfers if they were not following proper surfer etiquette. If the bad behavior persisted, Derek was known to swim by and snap off a fin or two for good measure. Everyone was happy when the "Sheriff of Backwash Bay" was in the area.

Another surfer who was often on Pollo's mind was Felipe, one of the three cool cats.

Felipe

Felipe was a goofy foot, just like Pollo, but he was well respected in the Matapalo lineup. No one offered any complaint about Felipe's surfing style. With his powerful paddling techniques, combined with his aggressive frontside cutbacks, Felipe felt right at home as a goofy foot riding the right-handers of Matapalo. Whether riding a longboard or a short board, Felipe dominated the lineup. No one was laughing at Felipe!

Felipe going backside at Backwash

Why was this not possible for Pollo? What was so wrong with his style that none of the other surfers included Pollo in their surfing sessions?

Pollo thought about it and came to a righteous conclusion. On the Pavones side, all the surfers had watched Pollo rip the long left-handers with style and grace. However, here in Matapalo, he had yet to even paddle out. He had no

51

reputation on this side of the Golfo Dulce. No one knew what he was capable of!

Pollo knew he needed to prove himself and he knew just where to start.

Pollo approached Mr. Bagley with tears in his eyes and said, "I am now ready. I want to learn to surf with style and grace, becoming one with these beautiful right-handers, and join the surfers of Matapalo in the lineup. Will you teach me, Mr. Bagley?"

Mr. Bagley smiled and handed Pollo a bar of wax. "*Polloson*," Mr. Bagley said, "if you want to learn to carve graceful lines with smooth, gliding transitions, surfing with style and power, you first must learn the art of waxing your board—wax on, wax off."

The Coati Kid's smile disappeared as he took the bar of wax. He didn't want to wax his surfboard! He wanted to paddle out and shred. His mood deepened as he repeatedly waxed the board and then stripped it off, muttering, "wax on, wax off." He felt like throwing the bar of wax into the sand as he watched Mako's groms erratically pumping and slashing with little to no style.

Wax on! Wax off!

Eventually, the Coati Kid scowled and demanded, "I thought you were going to teach me how to surf the right-handers. I want to go out and surf, and I want to go now!"

Mr. Bagley whispered, "*Polloson*, if you truly want to surf these right-handers with style and grace, you first must learn how to properly wax your board. Wax on, wax off."

The Coati Kid sighed, and muttered under his breath, "I know how to wax my board. I want to surf!" His smile was nowhere to be seen (no joy) as he waxed the board in broad, circular motions, and then stripped it off again.

As he reluctantly continued to "wax on, wax off," the Coati Kid watched as Mako's groms were surfing beautiful, clean waves, albeit with jerky and unconnected turns.

"Honestly, they look so ugly," Pollo thought to himself.

The Coati Kid protested out loud, "I want to surf the right-handers!"

Mr. Bagley calmly replied, "First you must learn to paddle out and paddle in. You must study tidal movement, currents, boils and back eddies, wind conditions, as well as timing larger sets. Most importantly, *Polloson*, you need to learn triangulation, for proper location in the lineup."

Pollo was totally frustrated. He simply wanted to go out, catch one of those right-handers, and show the surfers of Matapalo that he could rip.

Growing tired of seeing the clumsy groms totally abuse the waves at Backwash, the Coati Kid turned and peered out at Matachanchos as the Three Amigos—Aaron, Simón, and Kaliman—carved gracefully connected turns with powerful cutbacks, always looking for a barrel.

Pollo thought, "I can surf with style and grace just like them, but all Mr. Bagley wants me to do is mentally prepare, watch the tides and winds, and become completely familiar with my surroundings. And all I want to do is surf!"

Pollo paddling out

Pollo paddling in

For the next few weeks, with tears in his eyes, the Coati Kid reluctantly continued to "wax on, wax off," "paddle out and paddle in," all the while learning the magic of the ocean's movement.

He began to understand the clockwork precision of the tides. He knew how to read the boils that screamed, "danger, danger," giving warning to subsurface rock formations.

He was learning the art of triangulation, using Jimmy's rooftop, the vine-covered tree at Casa Tortuga and himself to form a perfect triangle, which allowed the Coati Kid to locate and maintain proper position in the lineup.

He was definitely beginning to understand the importance of watching and timing larger sets, having witnessed Mako getting sucked over the falls on numerous larger days.

Mako getting sucked over the falls

Day after day, the Coati Kid followed Mr. Bagley's instructions and continued, unknowingly, to get stronger and wiser.

Oh, how Pollo longed for the days of graceful gliding on the left-handers of Pavones, but he was beginning to see the wisdom of Mr. Bagley's training program. Soon, the Coati Kid would be ready!

Mako continued to make fun of Pollo and his waxing techniques, calling him a chicken as the Coati Kid continued to "wax on, wax off," "paddle out and paddle in," while looking around to calculate and maintain his position in the lineup. He studied tidal patterns while always watching for boils and hidden danger. He did all of this while never once stroking into a wave.

This was difficult for Pollo as Mako continued to harass him, but he persevered, and adhered to the strict guidelines laid out by Mr. Bagley.

The Coati Kid in Full Lotus

The Coati Kid continued to watch and time the larger sets. He knew the tidal cycle like the back of his paw, and triangulation was becoming second nature! His legs were becoming stronger by the day. Everything was coming together, and his confidence was building. He knew he could surf circles around Mako.

Finally, one morning, the Coati Kid mustered his courage and confided in Mr. Bagley. "I want to show Mako that I can carve graceful, connected turns, while making difficult sections and riding barrels. I want to master these right-handers!"

Mr. Bagley smiled and stuck his head into his shell for just a moment. When he reappeared, his smile was wider and happier than ever before. The turtle exclaimed with great excitement, "*Polloson*, you must now learn and master the legendary switch stance! You will drop-in backside, and carve a beautiful, deep and drawn-out bottom turn. Then, as you begin your trajectory up the face, you will perform the illusive switch stance with style and grace, positioning your body into the new and puzzling regular-foot stance while riding the surging right-hander."

"I am ready to surf NOW!" declared Pollo.

Mr. Bagley smiled and stuck his head back into his shell for a few minutes. When his head reappeared, his smile was deep and content. "*Polloson*, you first must master the beautiful switch stance *on dry land.*"

Pollo, the Coati Kid, felt like giving up. Nevertheless, he sighed and began practicing switching his stance on the sands of Pan Dulce.

Mako and his disciples callously laughed at the Coati Kid as he practiced the switch stance under the shade of an almond tree. However, Pollo knew that, out in the water, his friends were standing up for him. While in the lineup, both Charlies (Yoga Charlie and Texas Charlie) would take up for Pollo, pretty much putting Mako in his place every chance they could.

Yoga Charlie was one chicken who really knows his way around the waves. With his occasional no-paddle takeoffs, he was always turning heads as he caught more waves than any other surfer, with less effort and more style than all of Mako's groms put together. The Coati Kid would one day be able to surf with both Charlies, sharing waves at Backwash.

Texas Charlie had not only taught himself to fish with a rod and reel, but he also learned how to surf on a traditional longboard. His majestic wingspan was quite the propellant when charging down a smooth face at Backwash, and oh those long, drawn out bottom turns.

Pollo's mother enjoyed watching him practice his switch stance as she nibbled a few fresh almonds in the almond trees along the shoreline, squawking encouragement to him as he concentrated on his footwork and timing.

Pollo practicing "switch stance" while his MOM munches on almonds

For days, Pollo practiced and practiced, hour after hour, and soon he was able to perform the utilitarian switch stance with ease.

Pollo's legs were becoming stronger by the day. His board was professionally waxed, and the illusive switch stance now seemed like second nature. Pollo, the Coati Kid, knew that Mr. Bagley's wise training was coming to fruition, and it would soon be time to prove himself.

Chapter Four

The Coati Kid was unaware, but the magical day was rapidly approaching. The anticipated south swell (five to seven feet, 196 degrees, with 21 second periods) was filling in, and everyone lined up on the beach, their eyes popping out of their heads.

As the world spun, and the sun grew brighter above the mountains across Golfo Dulce, Mr. Bagley extended his neck and exposed his wise cranium toward the bright sunlight. He called out, "*Polloson*, today is the day! We will have the contest at Backwash Bay two hours before low tide."

The Coati Kid smiled in agreement and began his stretching exercises. Mako and his groms nervously watched as the new energy continued to roll through both Pollo and the ocean itself. Pollo continued to stretch as he watched for sets, calculating the timing while watching wind conditions.

The Coati Kid knew he was ready!

All the surfers in the bosque began to take their places for the competition.

Hippie Jim paddled around from Hog Hole and planned to watch the contest from outside. Jim was a cap-wearing turtle who had learned long ago to protect his cranium. Even a turtle can experience skin damage from the strength of the sun's rays, so Jim was never seen without his cap.

Phil paddled over from Seis Peces, while Darren grabbed a small papaya and settled into a high treetop. Derek swam into the lineup, and everyone else gathered on the beach.

Then, the contest horn sounded!

Mako and the Coati Kid grabbed their boards. Mako made a mad dash for the water and smirked as he paddled out. He was going to be the first one in the lineup, and surely the first one to catch a wave.

On the other hand, Pollo, the Coati Kid, took his time. He moved toward the shore break, but was sure to check the tide, test the wind, all while watching for big sets.

Mako did not concern himself with any of those details as he scratched for the horizon. He paddled furiously, wanting to catch the first wave of the contest. He was so excited; he was almost hyperventilating!

The Coati Kid stood silently at the shoreline, taking it all in. He watched as his mother gracefully circled overhead with B.D., who threatened to drop bombs on any unsportsmanlike contestants if necessary. Gretchen fluttered by and she watched Mr. Bagley swim out into the deeper water to witness the spectacle, acting as a secondary judge, just in case the contest results were disputed.

As the larger set rolled through, the Coati Kid watched as Mako struggled in the rip after taking three waves on the head. His rival had never bothered to master a clean paddle out, or a clean paddle in. He had not taken the time to check the conditions and had not looked for tidal movement or wind direction, and most importantly didn't watch for larger sets. The Coati Kid smiled as he thought of all the information and knowledge Mr. Bagley had bestowed upon him during his rigorous training.

Finally, the time was right. Pollo stroked out through calm waters, just as he had done so many times before. Sitting in the lineup, fresh and ready to go, the Coati Kid, who still had dry head fur, triangulated and watched as an exhausted Mako finally made it out.

Mako looked over and sneered at Pollo, who simply smiled and nodded.

Mako finally makes it out

The two surfers sat silently, waiting for the next set.

Looming on the horizon, the offshores were sculpting and manicuring the faces into open barrels. Pollo, the Coati Kid, knew his time had come.

As the set approached, Mako snaked Pollo and paddled for the first wave of the set. He was still exhausted from his haphazard paddle out, and it quickly became apparent that Mako was NOT going to catch the wave.

Disapproving of Mako's callous efforts, Andy gave a few powerful shakes of his tail while also reveling in what was about to happen.

The offshore winds blew, and it looked like rain coming off the crest of the wave. Just as he had practiced, the Coati Kid paddled out further, and was soon in perfect position to catch the sixth wave of the set. Pollo had triangulated and positioned himself exactly where he wanted to be.

Pollo waited for his wave, the best wave of the set. He stroked twice and the wave jacked heavily, and the Coati Kid instantly sprang to his paws, with the trough in front of him deepening and widening.

Mako, now caught inside, was taking his fourth wave on the head. He was being sucked dangerously closer and closer to the cheese grater as the Coati Kid began his descent down the beautifully sculpted face.

Dropping in backside, the Coati Kid set up for a long, drawn-out bottom turn. As he hit the apex, his fins carved a beautiful line, and his trajectory propelled him up the face. He realized it was time to utilize everything that Mr. Bagley had taught him.

The Coati Kid dropping in backside

With his weight shifting during his upward climb, Pollo performed the elusive switch stance. The crowd on the beach erupted into applause, a hoopin' and a hollerin', as the Coati Kid's body pivoted like a beautiful dancer. He had pulled off the legendary maneuver!

Pollo switching stance to "regular foot"

As he neared the top of this overhead, glassy wall, the Coati Kid began to cross-step to the nose like a *regular foot*. Gliding on the nose, trimming high on the sculpted face, Pollo knew that all his hard work was now paying off.

As the offshores manicured the feathering face, the Coati Kid knew it was time to switch back to goofy foot and perform the well anticipated frontside cutback, which he had seen Felipe do so many times before. The spectators on the beach once again erupted into thunderous applause, watching Pollo as he redirected his energy.

Mako, however, was now stuck in the rip, panic plastered all over his exhausted face. The cheese grater was looming dangerously closer.

Pollo, nearing the trough of the wave, carved a beautiful backside bottom turn. As he soared up the face, hitting the apex, the Coati Kid switched stance again back to regular foot. Racing along the face, in full trim, five claws over the nose, riding high on the naturally sculpted face, it was now the perfect opportunity to hang ten.

It was in that moment when Pollo spotted Mako in dire straits, about to be washed up and over the deadly cheese grater.

The Coati Kid spots Mako in trouble

Cross-stepping back, the Coati Kid switched his stance back to goofy foot and made a super aggressive frontside cut-back, throwing himself way out into the flats. The continuing thrust of his powerful cut-back propelled the Coati Kid within arm's reach of Mako.

The Coati Kid rescuing Mako

As Pollo surfed toward Mako and the razor-sharp cheese grater, he knew what he had to do. The Coati Kid grabbed Mako by the back of his neck and thrust him back out into deeper water.

Mako, now safely away from the cheese grater, was able to swim around and make it to the beach, but all the attention was now focused on the Coati Kid.

Pollo finished his ride, and kicked out as the offshore-blown droplets tickled his face. Gliding down the smooth back, a shower of water droplets massaged his body, and he smiled. He had ridden the last wave of the set and was in no danger.

Pollo knew that Mr. Bagley's training had made all the difference, and now smiling his most satisfying smile ever, the Coati Kid paddled in, just as he had done so many times before!

Everyone on the beach ran toward Pollo and raised him high above their heads. Pollo, the Coati Kid, had finally proven himself and was now an established member of the Matapalo surfing community!

Glossary of Surfing Terms

Aerial: When both surfer and surfboard hit the lip of the wave, at high speed, and launch off into the air.

A to B: describing a surfer who basically surfs straight down the wave with few to no cutbacks

Back in the hook: the hook is the most critical part of the wave, often curve-shaped like a hook.

Barrel: The hollow part of a breaking wave, where there is a round, hollow space between the face of the wave and the lip of the wave as it curls over.

Boils: A circular pattern on the wave face, formed as a swell passes over a raised area on the bottom—usually a large rock or cluster of rocks. Boils are generally a red flag, as they indicate shallow water.

Cheese grater: rock formation at Backwash Bay that has razor sharp edges and is considered extremely dangerous.

Deep: The steepest part of the shoulder closest to the peak of the wave is considered the deepest part of the wave. Often when a surfer is "too deep," they are unable to drop into a wave without falling off of their board.

Dropping in: Someone with the right of way is either about to take off on a wave, or is already riding a wave, and you also take off on the same wave in front of him or her.

Foil surfing: A type of surfing where a hydrofoil lifts the surfboard above the surface of the water by a whole foot or more. People describe the sensation of foil surfing as if they're actually flying along the ocean.

Frontside cutback: One of the staple maneuvers in surfing. When a goofy foot performs a cut back with his back toward the wave

Glass: When the waves (and general surface of the water) are extremely smooth, not disturbed by wind.

Going off: A term to describe very good, consistent surf.

Goofy Foot: Someone who surfs with their right foot forward on the surfboard.

Grom: A shortened form of "grommet," a grom is a young surfer, typically under 15 years old. Typically reserved for particularly skillful or irritating young surfers.

Hang ten: When ten toes are hanging off the nose of the surfboard.

Hit the lip: Hitting the top of the wave after taking a bottom turn.

Hooting: Cheering on a fellow surfer

Left-hander: A wave that breaks (or peels) to the left from the point of view of the surfer riding the wave. This means that, when looking from the beach towards the ocean, the wave will appear as breaking towards the right.

Longboard: Generally considered any rounded-nose surfboard over eight feet long and twenty inches wide.

No-paddle takeoff: A technique also known as the Pop & Cork Method that advanced surfers use to catch waves with little to no paddling required. Not only does this conserve energy, but it also helps advanced surfers catch more waves.

Peak: The highest breaking point of a wave, and the point where the wave begins to break. From here, experienced surfers start in a wave, because that guarantees the longest ride on the wave.

Point break: The location where a wave breaks as it hits a point of land jutting out from the coastline.

Regular Foot: Someone who surfs with their left foot forward on the surfboard.

Right-hander: A wave that breaks to the right from the surfer's vantage point. On a right-hander, the surfer rides the wave to his right, which would look like the left to the people onshore.

Set waves: Waves that come in larger than the overall significant wave height of the day.

Shine it on: To ignore something or someone.

Short board: Range from about five to seven feet long, and have two to four fins, and an upturned tip (nose kick).

Shredding: The ability to have such control over your surfboard that you master turns over the sections of the wave with great confidence.

Snaking: Essentially, snaking means paddling around another surfer to give yourself the right of way over a wave. The right of way in surfing is always given to the surfer closest to the peak of the wave, so paddling in front of someone that has the right of way to give yourself the right of way instead, makes you a snake.

South swell: Swells generated by storms in the South Pacific near the tip of South America and Antarctica. South Pacific swells, also called Southern Hemisphere swells, travel thousands of miles across the ocean before breaking along the Costa Rican coast and can produce epic surf.

Stash and Slash: The surfer inserts, or "stashes," the surfboard into the hook (curve) of the incoming wave and waits for the board to be sucked up the face of the wave. The surfer then swims beneath the water's surface and leaps out of the water, landing on the board and pushing it down the rapidly cresting wave.

Surfing in the air: Also known as sky surfing, it is a type of skydiving and extreme sport in which the skydiver performs surfing-style aerobatics during freefall.

Switch stance: Being able to ride a surfboard comfortably in either a goofy foot or regular foot position.

Tube riding: A term used by surfers to describe riding well inside the curve or barrel of a finely shaped breaking wave.